GEOGRAPHY
CHALLENGE
190
Fun and Creative
Problems for Kids

LEVEL 2

Arnold Cheyney

GOOD YEAR BOOKS

are available for most basic curriculum subjects plus many enrichme
areas. For more Good Year Books, contact your local bookseller or
educational dealer. For a complete catalog with information about
other Good Year Books, please contact:

Good Year Books
P.O. Box 91858
Tucson, AZ 85752-1858
www.goodyearbooks.com

Copyright © 1996, 2005 Good Year Books. All rights reserved.
Printed in the United States of America.

ISBN: 1-59647-028-3

Illustrations: Slug Signorino
Design: Daniel Miedaner

Really?

Air is a mixture of many gases, including hydrogen, nitrogen, and oxygen.

What keeps air from leaving the Earth and going into space? What is the air that surrounds the Earth called?

gravity; atmosphere

Fact!

Russia, the Earth's largest country, covers over 160 longitudinal degrees of the Northern Hemisphere.

How many degrees of longitude are there? What are the approximate limits of Russian land in longitude?

360 degrees; from about 3°E to about 17°W longitude

4

Cool!

There is no larger bird on the Earth than the African ostrich. It can run 40 miles (64 kilometers) per hour.

The African ostrich grows 8 feet (2.4 meters) tall and can weigh 345 pounds (156 kilograms). Can it fly?

ou

5

Listen!

The Gulf Stream is a warm current of water beginning in the Caribbean Sea

Can you describe the route of the Gulf Stream?

6

it flows through the Gulf of Mexico, past Florida, past the eastern coast of the United States, and breaks up at the Grand Banks. (Some of it comes past Europe and west Africa and begins again in the western Caribbean.)

Look!

Bangladesh is on the shoreline of the Bay of Bengal.

Three large rivers flow through Bangladesh, making the rainy season dangerous and sometimes deadly. What are the three rivers?

Brahmaputra, Ganges, Meghna

Neat!

The compass was first developed in China.

Which direction does a compass needle point? Why would this be a useful invention?

magnetic north; will vary but should include that it helps people find the direction they want to go when there are no signs

Fact!

Earth's highest and most extensive mountain system borders the northern part of India, Nepal, and western China.

What is this mountain system called? What is the name of the region in China that is covered by this range?

the Himalayas; Tibet

Really?

One of Israel's holiest places is the Wailing Wall, which contains stones from the Temple of early biblical times.

Where is the Wailing Wall located?

East Jerusalem

10

Cool!

Lewis and Clark, U.S. Army officers, explored northwestern America from 1804 to 1806.

They traveled 8,000 miles (12,800 kilometers). Which president of the United States sent them on the expedition?

Thomas Jefferson

Look!

The capital of Japan is Tokyo.

How many islands make up Japan? Which island is Tokyo on? What two bodies of water are on its west and east coasts?

12

four; Honshu; Sea of Japan and Pacific Ocean

Neat!

The largest of Japan's islands is Honshu.

What are the other islands' names? Which one is the smallest? What countries border the Sea of Japan?

13

Hokkaido, Shikoku, Kyushu; Shikoku is the smallest; North and South Korea, China, Russia, Japan

Fact!

North and South Korea are located on the eastern side of the continent of Asia.

At what parallel line are they divided?

14

38th parallel of north latitude

Look!

Mongolia lies between Russia and China in Asia.

What desert covers much of Mongolia's southeast section? What is Mongolia's capital?

15

Gobi Desert; Ulaanbaatar

Fact!

The Himalaya Mountains cover much of the kingdom of Nepal.

What is the capital of Nepal? What countries border Nepal?

16

Kathmandu; India, China

Listen!

Saudi Arabia is mostly a vast desert but has large deposits of petroleum under its land.

Saudi Arabia is ruled by a king who is also the chief religious leader. What is his title as religious leader?

17

imam

Fact!

The island country of Singapore lies between the South China Sea and the Indian Ocean.

What two large islands lie to the west and east of Singapore? What countries are they part of?

Sumatra, part of Indonesia, to the west; Borneo, part of both Malaysia and Indonesia, to the east

18

Look!

Azerbaijan is a country in central Asia.

On what sea is Azerbaijan located?
What other countries have borders
on that sea?

19

*the Caspian Sea; Russia, Kazakhstan,
Turkmenistan, and Iran*

Listen!

Moldova has close ties to Romania through language, history, and culture.

What river forms Moldova's western border?

Prut River

20

Neat!

Ukraine's southern border is formed by the Black Sea and the Sea of Azov.

Much of the land in Ukraine is called steppes. What is a steppe?

21

vast grass-covered, treeless plains

Fact!

Poland's northern border is a body of water.

What is the name of this body of water? What other countries border Poland?

Baltic Sea; Lithuania, Belarus, Ukraine, Slovakia, Czech Republic, Germany, Russia

22

Cool!

The eggs, or roe, of the sturgeon fish are a delicacy in Russia.

What is the name of this delicacy? Have you ever tried it?

23

caviar; will vary

Fact!

Liechtenstein is a very tiny country in western Europe. Can you find it on a map?

What is Liechtenstein's capital? What countries surround it?

24

Vaduz; Austria, Switzerland

Look!

even Arab independent states form
federation called the United Arab
mirates.

ind the UAE on a map. What is its
pproximate latitude and longitude?

25

approximately 24°N, 54°E

Listen!

Albania is a country bordering the Adriatic Sea.

The capital of Albania is Tiranë. What country is directly west of Albania?

Italy

26

Fact!

ulgaria, in southeast Europe, shares s northern border with Romania nd its southern border with Greece nd Turkey.

/hat body of water is its eastern order? What countries form its vestern border?

27

Black Sea; Macedonia, Serbia and Montenegro

Really?

On a globe or map, the country of Italy looks like a large boot.

Find Italy on a map or globe. What is the name of the island at the tip of the "boot"?

28

Sicily

Look!

n Switzerland, rivers flow in many
lirections; the Rhine flows to the
Jorth Sea, the Rhône flows to the
Mediterranean Sea, and the Ticino
lows to the Adriatic Sea.

Vhich direction does each of these
ivers flow?

north, south, east

Fact!

France is bordered by Belgium, Luxembourg, Germany, Switzerland, Italy, and Spain.

What body of water forms part of its southern border? What bodies of water lie to its west?

Mediterranean Sea; Bay of Biscay and English Channel (parts of the Atlantic Ocean)

30

Fact!

he island of Great Britain contains
ngland, Scotland, and Wales.

/hat other country is included in the
nited Kingdom?

Northern Ireland

31

Who Knew?

On England's southeast coast are the white cliffs of Dover.

What are the cliffs composed of that makes them white?

chalk

32

Look!

The smallest of the countries that form the United Kingdom is Northern Ireland.

What is Northern Ireland's capital? What sea lies between Northern Ireland and the rest of the United Kingdom?

Belfast; Irish Sea

33

Really?

Bagpipes are musical instruments used in Scottish ceremonies.

How many different notes can be played on a bagpipe?

nine

34

Fact!

The country of Wales is situated on a wide peninsula on the west side of England.

What is the name of the mountain chain running north to south in Wales?

Cambrian Mountains

Look!

The capital of Greece is Athens.

Islands make up about 20 percent of Greece. What three large seas surround the lower part of Greece?

Aegean Sea, Mediterranean Sea, Ionian Sea

36

Cool!

To the southeast of Greenland in the North Atlantic Ocean is the island country of Iceland.

Why is Iceland called a land of "midnight sun"?

Iceland has almost 24 hours of daylight in June, 24 hours of darkness in December

Listen!

The three land regions of Switzerland are the Jura Mountains, Swiss Plateau, and Swiss Alps.

What are Switzerland's four languages?

German, French, Italian, Romansch

38

Look!

The driest part of Israel is the Negev Desert.

Which of Israel's rivers is the longest?

Jordan River

Listen!

Portugal is on the Iberian Peninsula at its western side.

What country borders Portugal on its north and east? What other countries have Portuguese as an official language?

Spain; Angola, Brazil, Cape Verde, Guinea-Bissau, Mozambique, São Tomé and Príncipe

Listen!

Andorra is a small country in the Pyrenees Mountains. It is bordered by France to the north and Spain to the south.

The people of Andorra speak Catalan, a Romance language. What are other Romance languages?

Italian, French, Portuguese, Romanian, Spanish, Provençal, and Rhaeto-Romance

Fact!

Norway is a long, narrow country on the northwest edge of Europe.

Narrow inlets along the coast make fine harbors. What do Norwegians call these inlets?

fjords

42

Really?

More sugar beets are grown in Ukraine than anywhere else on the Earth.

What eastern European soup is made from beets?

43

borscht

In 1939, Thailand changed its name from Siam to Thailand.

What is the capital of Thailand?

Bangkok

Fact!

The west coast of Myanmar lies on the Bay of Bengal above the Indian Ocean.

What is the name of Myanmar's capital? What was Myanmar's old name?

45

Rangoon; Burma

geography challenge

Level 2

Listen!

Baghdad is both the capital of Iraq and its largest city.

What famous river is Baghdad located on? What is Iraq's chief resource?

Tigris; petroleum

46

Look!

The capital of Djibouti has the same name as the country.

What country lies across the water from Djibouti? What is the name of the two bodies of water that border Djibouti?

Yemen; the Red Sea and Gulf of Aden

47

Look!

The capital of Syria is Damascus.

What body of water forms Syria's western border?

Mediterranean Sea

48

Really?

Equatorial Guinea is partly on the continent of Africa and partly on five offshore islands.

The capital is on an island, Bioko, in the Gulf of Guinea. What is the name of the capital?

49

Malabo

Who Knew?

Level 2 — geography challenge

The Democratic Republic of the Congo, a large country just below the equator on the African continent, has a large percentage of Africa's rain forest.

What other continent has a major percentage of the world's rain forest?

South America

50

Neat!

A mountain country, Lesotho is completely surrounded by the Republic of South Africa.

What is Lesotho called because of its mountain scenery?

51

the Switzerland of Southern Africa

Fact!

Liberia, on the west coast of Africa, gets it name from Latin, meaning free land

Which United States president is the capital named for?

James Monroe

52

Listen!

São Tomé and Principe are two main islands forming one country in Africa off the western coast.

The islands were formed from volcanoes that are now extinct. What does *extinct* mean?

53

no longer active

Fact!

The African country extending farthes[t] west on the continent is Senegal.

The capital and largest city is Dakar. What ocean forms the western border[?]

Atlantic

54

Look!

Seychelles is an African country of about 90 islands lying in the Indian Ocean.

The majority of the people live on the island of Mahé where the capital is located. What is the capital?

55

Victoria

Look!

The capital of the African country of Sudan is Khartoum.

What is the main river of Sudan and into what country does it flow?

Nile River; Egypt

56

Fact!

Tanzania, in Africa, borders the Indian Ocean. Part of the country is located on islands in the Indian Ocean.

What are the names of the two largest islands of Tanzania?

57

Zanzibar and Pemba

geography challenge

Level 2

Listen!

In the center of southern Africa lies the country of Botswana.

What is the official language of Botswana? What country is west of Botswana? What country is south of it

58

English; Namibia; South Africa

Fact!

Burundi, in Africa, has a land area of 10,747 square miles (27,834 square kilometers). The state of Maryland has a land area of 10,455 square miles (27,077 square kilometers).

Which has the larger land area? By how much?

59

Burundi; by 292 square miles (757 square kilometers)

Really?

Gambia is a small, independent country surrounded by Senegal.

Gambia is only 30 miles (48 kilometers) wide. On what ocean is its capital located?

60

Atlantic Ocean

Fact!

Kenya is an African country on the east coast of the continent.

What ocean borders Kenya? What five countries border Kenya?

61

Indian Ocean; Sudan, Ethiopia, Somalia, Uganda, Tanzania

Really?

The official name of Morocco is the Kingdom of Morocco.

What is Morocco's largest city? What continent is Morocco part of?

62

Casablanca; Africa

Look!

he international boundary between
he United States and Canada runs
etween the two waterfalls at
iagara Falls.

low much water runs over the two
lls every second? What is the name
f the boat that
kes sightseers up
 see the falls?

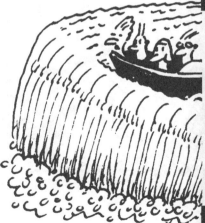

63

*about 100,000 cubic feet a second (during
the tourist season); the Maid of the Mist*

Fact!

The Appalachian Mountains, the second largest system of mountains in North America, extend from the Canadian province of Quebec to central Alabama.

Approximately how many miles long is the Appalachian Mountain chain?

approximately 1,500 miles (2,400 kilometers)

64

Cool!

The longest footpath in the United States is the Appalachian National Scenic Trail.

How long is the Appalachian National Scenic Trail? In what states does it begin and end?

65

2,000 miles (3,200 kilometers); Maine and Georgia

Neat!

Geysers shoot water into the air and volcanoes spew out melted (molten) rock.

What happens to water from geysers?

What happens to molten rock from volcanoes?

water from geysers evaporates or returns into the Earth; molten rock cools and becomes hard

Who Knew?

Petroleum is very useful stuff! We make aspirin, toothpaste, carpets, detergents, plastics, paint, and many other products from petroleum.

What country exports the most petroleum?

67

Saudi Arabia

Really?

Most tidal waves begin in places where earthquakes are relatively frequent, such as Japan, Alaska, and Chile.

Find Alaska, Chile, and Japan on a map or globe. What ocean do they have in common?

Pacific Ocean

68

Look!

Tidal waves are caused by shifts of the earth under the ocean or by hurricanes at sea.

What is the Japanese word for tidal wave?

69

tsunami

Fact!

There are approximately 455 active volcanoes on the Earth.

Several hundred of these volcanoes are called the Ring of Fire. Around what ocean is the Ring of Fire located?

Pacific Ocean

Really?

Storms with winds over 74 miles (119 kilometers) per hour in the Atlantic or eastern Pacific Ocean are called hurricanes.

What are hurricanes called in the western Pacific and Indian Oceans? What are they called off Australia?

71

typhoons; cyclones; willy-willies

Cool!

The moon travels around the Earth through space, and its gravitational force pulls up large bodies of water and lowers them, creating tides.

What are the two kinds of tides?

72

high and low tides

Look!

The highest mountain in North America is Denali (formerly Mount McKinley): 20,320 feet (6,194 meters).

Where is Denali located?

Alaska

Fact!

The two kinds of glaciers are continental glaciers and valley glaciers.

Valley glaciers are found in Alaska. Greenland and Antarctica have continental glaciers. What is the difference?

valley glaciers form in river valleys,
continental glaciers form on very cold
continents

74

Look!

At Point Barrow, Alaska, from May to August the residents have sunlight 24 hours a day.

Find Point Barrow, Alaska, on a map or globe. Why are the days so long in northern Alaska?

75

the tilt of the Earth on its axis causes the North Pole to slant toward the sun during summer

Neat!

The Himalayas are the highest system of mountains on the Earth.

The Himalayas separate the Tibetan Plateau from what large country? What country is Tibet a part of?

India; China

Fact!

Natural vegetation on the Earth is of four kinds: grassland, forest, desert shrub, and tundra.

What are the three types of grasslands?

77

steppes (short grasses), prairies (long grasses), tropical savannas (coarse grasses)

Look!

Istanbul, Turkey, is the only major city on the Earth that has parts on two continents.

On what two continents is Istanbul located?

Europe and Asia

78

Listen!

Acid rain is rain, snow, and sleet polluted with acids such as sulfuric and nitric acids.

What does acid rain pollute? Where is acid rain the biggest problem?

79

living organisms in lakes, rivers, streams, forests, soil, crops, etc.;
Europe

Indonesia is an island country of more than 13,600 islands.

Indonesia lies just south of Malaysia and north and west of Australia. What is Indonesia's capital?

Jakarta

Really?

The only lizards known to get their food from the ocean live on the Galapagos Islands.

What are these lizards called?

iguanas

81

Who Knew?

Meteor Crater, in Arizona, was made by a meteor that formed a hole 4,150 feet (1,245 meters) wide and 570 feet (171 meters) deep.

What is the closest city to the crater? What river runs by it?

Winslow; Little Colorado River

82

Look!

Guam, a territory of the United States, is the largest and most southern of the Mariana Islands in the western Pacific Ocean.

Find Guam on a map or globe. What is its capital?

83

Agana

Really?

Hawaii is the only state of the United States not on the North American continent.

What state of the United States is the farthest south?

Hawaii!

84

Look!

Puerto Rico is a United States commonwealth in the Caribbean Sea, north of Venezuela.

On a map, find the cities of San Juan and Mayagüez. Which city is on the west coast? Which is on the north coast?

85

Mayagüez is on the west coast; San Juan, the capital, is on the north coast

Cool!

Walt Disney World is near Orlando, Florida. It contains the Magic Kingdom, EPCOT, and the Disney-MGM Studios Theme Park.

What coast of Florida is Orlando closest to?

86

east coast

Fact!

The largest state east of the Mississippi is Georgia.

What is the capital and largest city in Georgia? What river runs by it?

Atlanta; the Chattahoochee River

87

Neat!

Georgia grows more peanuts than any other state in the United States.

What is one of the nicknames for Georgia? Which president of the United States was from Georgia?

Goober State; Jimmy Carter

Look!

The Mississippi River flows through the state of Louisiana.

Into what body of water does it flow? What famous Louisiana cities are located on the Mississippi?

89

the Gulf of Mexico; Baton Rouge, New Orleans

Weird!

The Pascagoula River in the state of Mississippi makes a sound similar to a swarm of flying bees.

What two cities flank the mouth of the Pascagoula on the Gulf of Mexico?

Gautier and Pascagoula (also Moss Point)

90

Fact!

he largest forest planted by humans
n the United States is in Nebraska:
2,000 acres (8,900 hectares).

n acre is 4,840 square yards. How
nany square feet make up one acre?
hint: 9 square feet = 1 square yard)

91

43,560

Really?

Minnesota is known as the "land of ten thousand lakes," although it actually has over 20,000.

What are the Twin Cities in Minnesota? Which has the higher population? Which is the capital?

Minneapolis/St. Paul; Minneapolis; St. Paul

Fact!

In the mid-1800s, many people traveled over 2,000 miles (3,200 kilometers) across the United States on the Oregon Trail.

What states did the Oregon Trail go through?

93

Missouri, Kansas, Nebraska, Wyoming, Idaho, Oregon

Fact!

The Chesapeake Bay, on the eastern coast of the United States, is located in Virginia and up through Maryland.

The bay is actually an estuary. What is an estuary?

a submerged river valley

94

Look!

The massive granite deposits in New Hampshire are the reason for calling the state the Granite State.

What kind of rock is granite? What are the two other kinds of rocks?

igneous; metamorphic, sedimentary

Neat!

In 1581, Spanish settlers created a road called El Camino Real (the royal highway) from Santa Fe, New Mexico to Mexico City, Mexico.

About how many miles (kilometers) long was the road?

about 1,300 miles (about 2,000 kilometers)

96

Fact!

Wisconsin is bordered by four states and two of the Great Lakes.

What are the states and lakes bordering Wisconsin?

97

Illinois, Iowa, Minnesota, Michigan; Lake Superior, Lake Michigan

Fact!

The Strait of Belle Isle divides Newfoundland from its northern part, Labrador.

What are the names of the two islands owned by France just a few miles south of Newfoundland?

St. Pierre and Miquelon

Really?

The Bay of Fundy, between Nova Scotia and New Brunswick, Canada, has the highest tides on the Earth.

The difference between high and low tide may be 50 feet (15 meters). How many of you would it take to be that high?

divide 50 feet by your height

Look!

The largest province in Canada is Quebec. About 55 percent of the province is forest.

Quebec has more freshwater rivers and lakes than any other province. What is the main river of Quebec?

St. Lawrence River

Who Knew?

The only seaport in the Canadian prairie provinces is Churchill, Manitoba.

What body of water is the port on?

Hudson Bay

Fact!

The province of Manitoba, Canada, is one of the three prairie provinces.

What are the other two Canadian prairie provinces?

Alberta, Saskatchewan

Really?

The Bahamas are a chain of 3,000 islands and reefs, only about 20 of which have people living on them.

Christopher Columbus landed on the island of San Salvador in the Bahamas on his first voyage. What year did this occur?

1492

103

Fact!

There are two sets of Virgin Islands:
The United States and the British.

What three islands in the Virgin Islands
are United States possessions?

St. Croix, St. John, St. Thomas

104

Fact!

The Lesser Antilles are a group of islands in the Caribbean Sea. There are two groups of islands that make up the Lesser Antilles.

What are the names of these two groups?

the Leeward Islands and the Windward Islands

Look!

Nicaragua is a country in Central America between Honduras and Costa Rica.

What is the capital of Nicaragua?
What is Nicaragua's east coast called?

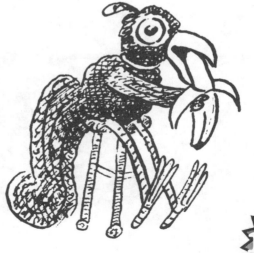

Managua; Mosquito Coast

Listen!

The most important export of Trinidad and Tobago is petroleum.

How far off the coast of the continent of South America is Trinidad?

CHAPPED STUCK

107

7 miles

Fact!

Part of the border between Argentina and Brazil is the Iguaçu River.

What other river separates Argentina from Brazil?

the Uruguay River

108

Really?

Bolivia in South America has three official languages.

What are the three official languages of Bolivia?

Spanish, Aymara, and Quechua

Fact!

The long, narrow country running down the west coast of South America is Chile.

How long is Chile?

2,650 miles (4,265 kilometers)

110

Really?

Colombia is the only country on the continent of South America to have a border on two different large bodies of water.

What are the two bodies of water?

Caribbean Sea and Pacific Ocean

Neat!

Coffee is a leading export from Colombia.

In the cold mountains, Colombians wear *ruanas* made from wool. What is a *ruana?*

blanket slit in the center to go over the head; poncho

112

Fact!

Co-operative Republic of Guyana is the official name of Guyana in South America.

What ocean forms its northern border?

Atlantic Ocean

113

Listen!

The smallest independent country in South America in area and population is Suriname (also spelled Surinam).

About what percentage of the country is forest?

114

about 80 percent

Look!

The capital of Uruguay is Montevideo.

What two countries and what ocean border Uruguay?

Brazil, Argentina, and the
Atlantic Ocean

Listen!

Burkina Faso is a country in western Africa surrounded by Niger, Benin, Togo, Ghana, Ivory Coast, and Mali.

What does the name Burkina Faso mean? What is the name of its capital?

HONKA

land of honest people; Ouagadougou

116

Weird!

Sleeping sickness, a disease spread by the tsetse fly, occurs in Africa and Asia.

Parasites carrying the disease live in animals as well as people. What is the name of the parasites that carry the disease?

117

trypanosomes

Look!

Comoros is an African country of four main islands and a few smaller ones.

What is the name of the large island southeast of Comoros?

118

Madagascar

Listen!

Poor rural peasants living in Egypt are called *Fellahin.*

What are nomadic desert herdsmen called?

119

Bedouins

Who Knew?

The official religion of Egypt is Islam and Arabic is its official language. Cairo, the capital, is the largest city in Africa.

What famous ancient Egyptian buildings still survive today?

the pyramids

Really?

Africa's Ivory Coast (Côte d'Ivoire) was named by French sailors who traded for ivory there.

What does ivory come from? The ivory trade is now outlawed. Why?

elephant tusks; elephants were killed just for their tusks

Fact!

Nairobi is the capital of Kenya, a country in Africa.

Africa's tallest mountain is across Kenya's border in Tanzania. What is its name?

Mt. Kilimanjaro

122

Listen!

Swahili is an official language of Kenya and other countries along the east coast of Africa.

What is the other official language of Kenya?

123

English

Fact!

Monrovia, the capital of Liberia, was named for President James Monroe, the fifth president of the United States.

Monrovia is on the coast of Liberia at the mouth of what river?

St. Paul

124

Look!

The fourth largest island on the Earth is Madagascar, off the southeastern coast of the continent of Africa.

What islands are larger than Madagascar?

Greenland, New Guinea, Borneo

Fact!

The country of Morocco has its borders on the Mediterranean Sea and the Atlantic Ocean.

What is the name of the strait separating it from the European continent?

126

Strait of Gibraltar

Fact!

Somalia is on the east coast of Africa. Its capital is Mogadishu.

What gulf is to its north? What ocean is to its south?

127

Gulf of Aden; Indian Ocean

Really?

South Africa has three capitals, one for each branch of government: legislative, administrative, and judicial.

What are the three capitals? What branch does each represent?

Cape Town (legislative), Pretoria (administrative), Bloemfontein (judicial)

Look!

Swaziland is surrounded by South Africa on three sides. Mozambique is on its eastern border.

What other small country is surrounded by South Africa?

129

Lesotho

Fact!

The country farthest north on the continent of Africa is Tunisia. Tunisia is between Algeria and Libya.

What is Tunisia's northern border?

the Mediterranean Sea

130

Neat!

In the middle of Africa is the country of Democratic Republic of the Congo. A third of the country is covered by tropical rain forest.

Part of the country borders the Atlantic Ocean. What countries are to the north and south of this border?

Angola, Republic of the Congo

131

Afghanistan is a country in central Asia above the Arabian Sea.

What five countries border Afghanistan?

Turkmenistan, Uzbekistan, Tajikistan, Pakistan, Iran

Listen!

Bhutan is a small country surrounded by India and China. The people of Bhutan speak a Tibetan dialect called Dzongkha.

What mountain range is Bhutan located on?

133

the Himalayas

Fact!

Brunei, a country in southeast Asia, is surrounded by part of Malaysia on the island of Borneo.

What other country is located partly on Borneo?

Indonesia

Listen!

Cambodia shares borders with Thailand, Laos, and Vietnam. A large number of the people are from a group called Khmer.

What body of water is to the west of Cambodia?

135

Gulf of Thailand

Weird!

India, with the second largest population on the Earth, has 16 official languages: Hindi, English, Sanskrit, and 13 regional languages.

What country has a larger population?

China

136

Cool!

Lemurs, a kind of primitive primate, live only in the island country of Madagascar. There are about 16 species of lemur.

What country is west of Madagascar across the water? What ocean is Madagascar in?

Mozambique; Indian Ocean

Neat!

The ruins of the ancient cities of Nineveh and Babylon are in Iraq.

The Earth's first known civilization developed in Iraq between two well-known rivers. What are they?

138

Tigris and Euphrates

Really?

On May 14, 1948, Israel became a country and the homeland for Jews scattered all over the Earth.

What countries border Israel? What body of water forms its other border?

139

Lebanon, Syria, Jordan, Egypt; the Mediterranean Sea

Look!

One of the most highly populated island countries on the Earth is Japan. Japan is made up of four large islands and thousands of smaller ones.

What are the four largest islands of Japan?

Hokkaido, Honshu, Kyushu, Shikoku

140

Maldives is the smallest independent country in Asia. Maldives is made up of 1,200 islands in the Indian Ocean.

What is its nearest large country?

MALDIVES OR BUST

141

India

Look!

Oman is located on the eastern tip of the Saudi Arabian peninsula, bordered to the east by the Gulf of Oman and the Arabian Sea.

What is the name of the strait just north of the northern tip of Oman?

Strait of Hormuz

142

Fact!

Pakistan lies on the northern coast of the Arabian Sea between Iran and India. Afghanistan forms part of its northern border.

To what religious faith do most Pakistanis belong?

143

Islam

Look!

The Philippines is a country made up of more than 7,000 islands north of Indonesia.

What are the two largest islands in the Philippines? What sea is located between the Philippines and Malaysia?

Luzon and Mindanao; the Sulu Sea

Fact!

Qatar is a small peninsular country jutting into the Persian Gulf.

Qatar's economy is based on oil production. When was oil discovered in Qatar?

145

1939

Really?

Two of the holiest cities in the Muslim world are in Saudi Arabia.

What are the names of these two cities?

Mecca and Medina

146

Listen!

Taiwan is an island in the South China Sea. The Chinese National government relocated there after the Chinese Communists took over in 1949.

What is the strait called that lies between mainland China and Taiwan?

147

Formosa Strait

Fact!

Turkey is a Middle Eastern country in Europe and Asia. Most of Turkey lies in Asia.

What is the name of the section of Turkey located in Europe?

148

Thrace

Look!

Armenia lies in the Caucasus Mountains surrounded by Azerbaijan, Iran, Turkey, and Georgia.

What two large bodies of water are to its east and west?

Caspian Sea, Black Sea

Fact!

Georgia is a country whose western border is the Black Sea.

What countries and republics border Georgia? What sea is about 130 miles (200 kilometers) east of Georgia?

Russia, Azerbaijan, Armenia, Turkey; Caspian Sea

150

Listen!

The people of Turkmenistan speak a language called Turkmen as well as Russian.

More than 80 percent of the country is covered by desert. What is the name of the desert?

151

Kara-Kum Desert

Look!

Kyrgyzstan is a mountainous country whose capital is Bishkek.

Sheep are important to the economy of Kyrgyzstan's people. What importal things come from sheep?

may include: wool, lanolin

Neat!

Malta is an independent island country south of Sicily in the Mediterranean Sea.

There are 2,943 people per square mile (1,136 per square kilometer) in Malta. How does that compare with your city or country?

divide number of people by square miles or square kilometers

Cool!

A large part of Russia (75 percent) is a region called Siberia.

What mountain range forms Siberia's western border?

Ural Mountains

154

Listen!

Yemen is a country southwest of Saudi Arabia. Its full name is Al Jumhuriyah al Yamaniyah (the Republic of Yemen).

What countries and bodies of water border Yemen?

Saudi Arabia, Oman, Red Sea, Gulf of Aden, and Arabian Sea

Look!

Italy is surrounded on three sides by seas.

What are the seas that surround Italy?

Adriatic, Mediterranean, Tyrrhenian, Ligurian, Ionian

156

Fact!

From 1918 until 1992, Czechoslovakia was one country.

Czechoslovakia has since been divided into two countries. What are they?

157

Czech Republic and Slovakia

Fact!

Germany is in central Europe.

What nine countries border on Germany?

Poland, Czech Republic, Austria, Switzerland, Luxembourg, Belgium, Netherlands, Denmark, and France

158

Who Knew?

Portugal has two outlying territories. They are island groups southwest of it in the Atlantic.

What are the names of these territories?

159

Azores, Madeiras

Fact!

Austria, in central Europe, is noted for its beautiful mountain scenery.

Eight countries border Austria. Can you name them?

Germany, Czech Republic, Slovakia, Hungary, Slovenia, Italy, Switzerland, and Liechtenstein

160

Look!

The Kölen Mountains separate Norway and Sweden in the north.

What is the name of the gulf that separates Sweden and Finland?

161

Gulf of Bothnia

Really?

Denmark is a country in the north of Europe made up of a peninsula and 482 islands.

What is the peninsula called?

162

Jutland

Fact!

Finland is bordered on its west by Sweden, north by Norway, and east by Russia.

Sweden and Russia battled for Finland for a thousand years. When did Finland declare its independence?

163

1917

Cool!

The Tour de France, an annual 30-day bicycle race throughout France, ends in Paris each summer.

What famous tower is located in Paris?

the Eiffel Tower

164

Look!

The Loire River, which is 650 miles (1,050 kilometers) long, is the longest river in France.

What is the name of the river flowing through Paris?

165

Seine River

Neat!

If Mount Everest could be dropped into the deepest part of the ocean, the Mariana Trench, it would not break the water's surface.

How far below the surface of the ocean would Mount Everest be?

166

over one mile (1.6 kilometers)

Fact!

Corsica is a French island in the Mediterranean Sea southeast of France.

What is the name of the island nine miles south of Corsica? To what country does this island belong?

167

Sardinia; Italy

Really?

Polders, areas drained of water, in the Netherlands have added 710 square miles (1,838 square kilometers) to the country.

The Dutch began the development of polders in A.D. 1300. How many centuries ago was that?

over six centuries

Listen!

Wales is a large peninsula bordering England along its east side. Welsh and English are spoken there.

What country is directly west of Wales?

169

Ireland

Cool!

Ports on the southern coast of
Iceland are open all year round,
despite its very northern location.

What water system
keeps southern
Iceland's ports
from freezing
over in the
winter?

*the Gulf Stream flows by the southern
coast of Iceland*

Look!

Liechtenstein, in Europe, is one of the smallest countries on the Earth at 62 square miles (160 square kilometers).

What two European countries are smaller than Liechtenstein?

171

Monaco, San Marino

Neat!

Marco Polo, an Italian explorer (1271–1295), traveled to Sri Lanka, China, India, Iran, and Sumatra.

What country is the island of Sumatra a part of?

172

Indonesia

Fact!

Lapland is a region above the Arctic Circle that covers Norway, Sweden, Finland, and Russia.

What group of Lapps raise reindeer for their livelihood?

173

Mountain Lapps

Look!

The peninsula in northern Europe made up of Norway and Sweden is called Scandinavia.

What country is located across the Gulf of Bothnia from Scandinavia?

Finland

174

Fact!

A strait is a narrow waterway connecting two larger bodies of water.

What two bodies of water does the Strait of Gibralter connect? What continents does it separate? What countries are on either side?

Atlantic Ocean and Mediterranean Sea; Europe and Africa; Spain and Morocco

Cool!

Of the Earth's natural resources, some are renewable, others are not. Solar energy and wind power are examples of renewable resources.

What nonrenewable resources do you know of? What do we do to conserve them?

fossil fuels, like oil and coal; we try to use less and substitute renewable resources when we can

Listen!

The San Andreas Fault in California is the site of numerous recent earthquakes.

What two plates are sliding along each other at the San Andreas Fault?

the Pacific plate and the North American plate

Fact!

There are three different kinds of plate boundaries: converging, diverging, and shearing.

What results from each of these movements? Can you name an example of each?

converging plates form mountains and volcanoes (Himalayas); diverging plates cause rifts in the ocean floor (Mariana Trench); shearing plates cause tremors (San Andreas Fault)

178

Really?

Many countries' flags contain similar symbols or use similar color patterns.

What two countries' flags have green, white, and orange vertical stripes? What four countries' flags have green, white, and red horizontal stripes?

179

Côte d'Ivoire, Ireland; Bulgaria, Hungary, Somaliland, Tajikistan

Listen!

Floods can cause a lot of trouble for people who live or work nearby.

Flooding is worse in areas where the forest has been cut down. Why would cutting down forests increase flooding?

180

trees hold soil in place and absorb water

Neat!

Chocolate is made from cacao beans grown on trees found on the west coast of Africa and in the country of Brazil.

What are some of Brazil's other important products?

may include: iron, steel, coffee, soybeans

Fact!

The first people to sail the length of the Mediterranean Sea were the Phoenicians in 1100 B.C.

What countries are at the east and west ends of the Mediterranean Sea?

182

Spain, Morocco; Syria, Lebanon, Israel

Really?

The largest island on the Earth is Greenland: 840,004 square miles (2,175,600 square kilometers).

Greenland is a province of what country?

Denmark

Neat!

One of the Seven Wonders of the Ancient World was the Lighthouse of Alexandria, Egypt, built in 283–246 B.C.

A fire burned at the top of the marble structure for illumination. What are lighthouses used for?

Out of Order

warn ships they are nearing land, warn of rocks and reefs, determine a ship's position

184

Who Knew?

The oldest Spanish fort in North America is in St. Augustine, Florida.

What is the fort called? In what year was it built?

185

Castillo de San Marcos; 1565

Listen!

Alamogordo, New Mexico, was the site of the first test of an atomic bomb explosion.

Where did the atomic bombs explode in World War II?

186

Hiroshima and Nagasaki, Japan

Look!

Cape Hatteras, off the North Carolina coast, became known as the Graveyard of the Atlantic because of the many shipwrecks there.

Find Cape Hatteras on a map. Is it connected by land to the mainland of North Carolina?

ou

Weird!

The oldest known dugout canoe, buil⁺ in 1600 B.C., was found in a peat bog in Ashland County, Ohio.

What does B.C. mean? How many years ago was it that the canoe was built?

before the birth of Christ; add 1,600 to the present year

Fact!

Kingston is the capital and chief port of Jamaica.

Jamaica is a leader in producing bauxite. What metal is made from bauxite?

189

aluminum

Look!

The country of Niger on the African continent has no outlet to the sea. The country was named for the river that flows through it.

What state in the United States has the same name as the U.S.'s longest river?

Mississippi

Fact!

The Philippines were named after a King of Spain, King Philip II.

What is the capital of the Philippines? On which island is it located?

Manila; Luzon

Cool!

The first people to sail the length of the Mediterranean Sea were the Phoenicians in 1100 B.C.

What countries are at the east and west ends of the Mediterranean Se

Spain, Morocco; Syria, Lebanon, Israel

192